MW01009756

MOUNT HOOD

THE HEART OF OREGON

Photography by **PETER MARBACH**

≈

Essay by **JANET COOK**

GRAPHIC ARTS BOOKS

To Lorena and Sofia, for your love and understanding of my passion for high places.

To my mother, Ethel, for the gifts of imagination, perseverance, and faith.

To all who cherish the mystery and grace of the mountain.

—PETER MARBACH

With love and gratitude to Mom and Dad, and Peter and Tate.

—JANET COOK

ACKNOWLEDGMENTS

Special thanks to Gary Larsen and the Mt. Hood National Forest for your enthusiastic support
for this project. And to Providence St. Vincent's Heart and Vascular Institute, especially Dr. Jeffrey Swanson
and Lydia Hibsch, for your divinely timed support and for restoring my heart and soul. —P. M.

Photographs © MMV by Peter Marbach
Essay © MMV by Janet Cook

Library of Congress Cataloging-in-Publication Data
Marbach, Peter.
    Mt. Hood : the heart of Oregon / photography by Peter Marbach ; essay by
Janet Cook.
        p. cm.
    ISBN 1-55868-923-0 (hardbound : alk. paper)
    1. Hood, Mount (Or.)—Pictorial works. 2. Hood, Mount (Or.)—Description
and travel. 3. Mount Hood National Forest (Or.)—Pictorial works. 4. Mount
Hood National Forest (Or.)—Description and travel. I. Title: Mount Hood.
II. Cook, Janet, 1966–   III. Title.
    F882.H85M37 2005
    917.95'41—dc22   2005019448

Graphic Arts Books
An imprint of Graphic Arts Center Publishing Company
P.O. Box 10306, Portland, Oregon 97296-0306
503-226-2402; www.gacpc.com

President: Charles M. Hopkins
Associate Publisher: Douglas A. Pfeiffer
Editorial Staff: Timothy W. Frew, Tricia Brown, Kathy Howard, Jean Bond-Slaughter
Designer: Jean Andrews
Production Staff: Richard L. Owsiany, Vicki Knapton
Printed in China

FRONT COVER: Trillium Lake reflects Mount Hood with a cloud-dotted sky.
HALF-TITLE PAGE: The mountain stands high above a pasture near Parkdale.
TITLE PAGE: Vine maple at Lost Lake frames Mount Hood in fall colors.
▷ In the Columbia Wilderness Area, Eagle Creek receives Metlako Falls.
▷▷ At Timothy Lake, a quiet day of fishing provides restoration.

To the many partners in stewardship, in the name of the American public and the 4.5 million people each year who enjoy recreating on the Mt. Hood National Forest.

100 years in our forests . . .

In Wildness is the preservation of the World.
Every tree sends its fibers forth in search of the Wild . . .
. . . From the forest and wilderness come
the tonics and barks which brace mankind.
—Henry David Thoreau

Four and one-half million people visit Mt. Hood National Forest every year.

They enjoy the scenery, hike, visit historic sites—including Timberline Lodge—ski, picnic, camp, study nature, bicycle, boat, use snowmobiles and off-road vehicles, collect mushrooms, cut firewood, and find the family Christmas tree. In addition, many people make their living directly or indirectly from the Forest—including among many others, ski instructors, outfitter guides, and forest products and tourism workers.

I look with great pride to the enduring significance of National Forests to the American landscape and to the very character of the American people. I believe the hallmark of the next century of service will be citizens rising to redeem their stewardship responsibilities for the forests they love.

I believe we are at the beginning of an environmental renaissance marked by people who appreciate the beauty and recognize the importance of National Forests to our sustenance, to nurturing our spirits, and to our long-term well-being—people who care about protecting, conserving, restoring, teaching, and learning about natural resources.

Already the sprouts of a new way of doing business are taking root.

Not too many years ago, Mt. Hood National Forest employees were directly responsible for providing almost all of the services on which our millions of visitors depended. Today, we have made an almost complete shift to engaging permittees; concessionaires; volunteers; business partners; contractors; cooperating local, state, Tribal, and other federal agencies; and nongovernmental organizations of all kinds to deliver almost all the services to the American public.

ꙅ In commemoration of the Forest Service Centennial ꙅ

From the desk of
Gary L. Larsen
Forest Supervisor
Mt. Hood National Forest
2005

Mt. Hood National Forest Volunteers and Partners (2003–2005)

Ackerman Middle School
Adventures Without Limits
AGAPE Youth & Family Ministry
Airtouch Communications
Alder Creek Kayak Supply, Inc.
All Star Rafting, Inc.
Alpha School
Alpine Hut
Alpinist
American Alpine Institute
American Bird Conservancy
American Birding Association
American Diabetes Association
American Fisheries Society
American Hiking Society
AMERICORPS
Appleknockers
ANPO, inc.
Arbor School
Arrah Wanna Homeowner's Association
Associated Oregon Loggers
Association of Northwest Steelheaders
AT&T Wireless Services of Oregon
Audubon Society of Portland
Australian Center for Astrology
Autumn Festival Volunteers
Backcountry Horsemen of Oregon
Backyard Bird Snaps
Badger Improvement District
Bar G Ranch & Ride
Barlow Trail Long Rifles
Bend Metro Parks & Recreation
Birds of a Feather
Blue Sky Whitewater Rafting
Boise Cascade Corporation
Bonney Butte HawkWatch
Bonneville Power Administration
Boring Fire District
Boy Scouts of America, Pacific Northwest
    Council Troops & Columbia Pacific Council
Boys and Girls Club of America
Bridge Pedal, Inc.
British Columbia Ministry of Forests
Bureau of Land Management
Camera Crew
Camp Creek Water Association
Canby Fire District
Cascade Alliance
Cascade Dog Sled Club
Cascade Geographic Society
Cascade Utilities
Cascadia Wild!
Catlin Gabel School
Central Catholic High School
Century Telephone, Inc.
Church of Jesus Christ of Latter-day Saints
Clackamas Board of County Commissioners
Clackamas County Development Agency
Clackamas County Education,
    Training and Business Services
Clackamas County Environmental Youth Corps
Clackamas County Fire District #1
Clackamas County Fire Prevention Co-op

Clackamas County Service District
Clackamas County Sheriff
Clackamas County Soil and Water District
Clackamas County Tourism
    Development Council
Clackamas County Water
    Environment Services
Clackamas Lake Guard Station & Recreation
Clackamas River Basin Watershed Council
Clackamas River Water Providers
Cleveland High School
Coffee People
CogWild
Colton Fire District
Colton Telephone Company
Columbia Area Mountain Bike Advocates
    (CAMBA)
Columbia Gorge Power Sledders
Columbia Observed Trials
Columbia River Council of Girl Scouts
Confederated Tribes of Warm Springs
Cooper Spur Ski Area
Corbett Fire District
Corbett High School
Cornell University Labs
Crag Rats
Cub Scouts Pack 20—Guy Miller Tree Plant
Dairy Queen
Daniels & Associates, Inc.
David Douglas High School, Portland, Oregon
Deschutes Resources Conservancy
Destination Wilderness
Discovery Cycle
Douglas Water Power & Company
Dufur, City of
Eagle Creek National Fish Hatchery
Eagle Scout Project
Earthlink/UNAVCO
East Fork Irrigation District
Ecotours of Oregon
Escape Adventures, Inc.
Estacada Chamber of Commerce
Estacada High School
Estacada Natural History School
Estacada Rural Fire Dept. #69
Eugene Water & Electric Board
Faubian Summer Homes Association
Farmers Irrigation District
Federal Energy Regulatory Commission
Federal Highway Administration
Fifteenmile Watershed Council
Fir Mountain Ranch Outfitters, Inc.
Fire Volunteers
Fisheries Snorkel Assistance (Volunteers)
Fly Fishing Shop, The
Friends of Clackamas Lake Guard Station
Friends of Northwest Forests
Friends of Sandy River Cabin
Friends of Silcox Hut
Friends of Timberline
Gas Transmission Northwest Corporation
General Telephone Company
Girl Scouts
Gladstone Fire Department
Gorgefest
Gorge Fly Shop
Gorge Freeriders
Government Camp Historical Society
Government Camp Sanitary District
Government Camp Water Company

Grant High School
Gresham City Fire Department
Gresham City Parks Division
Gresham Fire District
GS Troop/Green Canyon
HawkWatch International
Heritage Learning Institute
Heritage Research & Associates, Inc.
Hoodland Fire District #74
Hoodland Thriftway
Hoodland Video
Hood River Cellular Telephone Company
Hood River County Board of Commissioners
Hood River County Community Corrections
Hood River County Juvenile Department
Hood River County Soil and
    Water Conservation District
Hood River Off-Road Association
Hood River Watershed Group
Hoodland Fire District
Hoyt Arboretum
Hurricane Racing
Hutch's Bicycle
Immigrant and Refugee Community Organization
Inner City Youth Institute
Institute for Bird Populations
International Mountain Biking Association
Izaak Walton League, Washington County Chapter
Johnson Creek Watershed Council
Julee's Gorge Tours
KGW, Northwest News Channel 8
KINK FM 102 Radio Station
Klamath Bird Observatory
KOIN-TV
Lady Creek Water System
Lake Oswego Fire Department
Leupold and Stevens
Lewis & Clark College
Lost Boulder Irrigators
Lost Lake Campground Complex Concessionaire
MacLaren Youth Correctional Facility
Majestics
Marion County Posse
Mazamas
McBain and Trush, Inc.
MCI Worldcom Network Services, Inc.
METRO
Mid-Columbia Council of Governments
Mid-Columbia Fire Prevention Co-op
Mid-Columbia Fire & Rescue
Middle Fork (Hood River) Irrigation District
Milwaukie Garden Club
Molalla Fire District
Molalla Water Providers
Mountain Quail Business Services
Mountain Shop
Mountain Signal Memorial Fund
Mountain View Cycle
MountainSavvy
Mt. Hood Area Chamber of Commerce
Mt. Hood Community College
Mt. Hood Cultural Center and Museum
Mt. Hood Cycling Classic
Mt. Hood Fire Prevention Association
Mt. Hood Foods
Mt. Hood Information Center
Mt. Hood Kiwanis Camp
Mt. Hood Management
Mt. Hood Meadows
Mt. Hood Roasters
Mt. Hood Ski Bowl
Mt. Hood Ski Patrol
Mt. Hood Snowmobile Club
Mt. Hood Summer Ski Camp

Mt. Hood Village Resort
Mt. Scott Motorcycle Club
Mt. View Cycle
Multnomah County Board of Commissioners
Multnomah County Department of
    Juvenile and Adult Community Justice
Multnomah County Parks
Multnomah County Youth Cooperative
National Fish and Wildlife Foundation
National Forest Foundation
National Marine Fisheries Service
National Oceanic and
    Atmospheric Administration
National Science Foundation
National Ski Patrol
Native Fish Society
Native Plant Society of Oregon
Natural Resources Conservation Service
Nature Conservancy, The
Nature's Northwest
North American Bird Conservation Initiative
Northwest Association of Fire Trainers
Northwest Discoveries
Northwest Ecological Research Institute (NERI)
Northwest Fly Fishers Club (7 Volunteers)
Northwest Interpretive Association
Northwest Nordic
Northwest School of Survival
Northwest Service Academy
Northwest Sportfishing Industry Association
Northwest Tour & Trail
Northwest Youth Corps
Olallie Campground Complex Concessionaire
Orchard Ridge Ditch Company
Oregon Archaeological Society
Oregon Bicycle Riders Association
Oregon Candy Farm
Oregon Department of Environmental Quality
Oregon Department of Fish and Wildlife
Oregon Department of Forestry
Oregon Department of Parks & Recreation
Oregon Department of Transportation
Oregon Episcopal School
Oregon Equestrian Trails
Oregon Games
Oregon Hunters Association
Oregon Muleskinners
Oregon Museum of Science and
    Industry Science Camp
Oregon National Guard
Oregon Nordic Club
Oregon Peak Adventures
Oregon Public Policy Dispute Resolution Program
Oregon River Experiences
Oregon Road Runners
Oregon State Adopt-A-River
Oregon State Federation of Garden Clubs
Oregon State Police
Oregon Tourism Commission
Oregon Trail School District
Oregon Trout
Oregon Youth Conservation Corp
Oregon Zoo
OSU Outdoor Footsteps Program
Pacific Coast Joint Venture
Pacific Crest Outward Bound School
Pacific Crest Trail Association—
    Mt. Hood Chapter
Paradise Trail Christian Camp
Parkdale Fire Department
Parkdale Sanitary
    District

Parkdale School
Partners-in-Flight
Pete's Pile Climbing Association
Pinnacle Towers, Inc.
Point Reyes Bird Observatory
Port of Portland
Portland, City of
Portland Coffee Roasters
Portland Fire District
Portland General Electric
Portland Mountain Rescue
Portland Parks & Recreation
Portland Post Office Club
Portland Public Schools
Portland Roasting Company
Portland State University
Portland Unit of Mountain Rescue
Portland United Mountain Pedalers (PUMP)
Portland Water Bureau
Powell Valley Long Rifles
Ptarmigans
Quest Corporation
Radio Shack
Reachout Expeditions
Reed College
Region 9 Education Service District
Recreational Equipment Inc.
Resort at the Mountain, The
Reynolds High School
Reynolds Learning Academy
Reynolds School District
Rhododendron Summer Homes
    Association
River Drifters White Water Tours
Riverkeeper (Restoration)
RLK & Company
Rock Creek District
    Improvement Company
Rocky Mountain Elk Foundation
Ruffed Grouse Society
Salmon Corps
Sand Mountain Society
Sandy Area Chamber of Commerce
Sandy Fire District
Sandy High School
Sandy River Basin Watershed Council
Sandy River Hatchery
Sierra Club
Singletrack Ranch
Skyline Hospital
Snowshoe Club
SOLV
Spawning Survey Assistance (1 Volunteer)
Sports Car Club of America, The
Sportsman's Park Water Association
Sprint Spectrum, L.P.
St. Mary's School
State Fire Marshall Office
Student Conservation Association
Subway
Sustainable Ecosystems Institute
Tanager Telecommunications, LLC
Teachers In The Woods
The Dalles, City of
The Dalles High School
    The Dalles Water Bureau
        The Dalles Watershed Council
            Timberlake Job Corps Center

oThousand Trails Management Services, Inc.
Timberline Lodge Volunteer Interpreters
Timberline Mountain Guides
T-Mobile USA, Inc.
Trails Club of Oregon
Travel Oregon
Trout Unlimited—Fishing Clinic
Trout Unlimited—Clackamas and Tualatin
Trust Management Services
Tualatin Hills Park & Recreation
Tualatin Valley Fire and Rescue
Tubbs Snowshoe—Romp & Stomp
UNAVCO Plate Boundary Observatory
U.S. Army Corps of Engineers
U.S. Fish and Wildlife Service
U.S. Geological Survey
U.S. Institute for Environmental
    Conflict Resolution
U.S. Marine Corps
U.S. Veterans Affairs, Department of
United Telephone Company of NW
University of Oregon School of Architecture
USDA Natural Resources
    Conservation Service
USDI Bureau of Land Management
Vancouver Parks & Recreation
Varsity BSA
Verizon Wireless, LLC
Village Store, The
Waldorf School
Wapinitia Home Owners Association
Wasco County Commission on
    Children and Families
Wasco County Court
Wasco County Public Works
Wasco County Sheriff and
    Juvenile Department
Wasco County Soil and
    Water Conservation District
Wasco County Youth Services
Wasco Electric Cooperative
Washington County 4-H Wagon Train
Washington Department of Fish & Wildlife
Washington Department of Natural Resources
Welches Mountain Building Supply
Welches School
West Cascades Chapter of
    The Backcountry Horsemen
Western Spirit Cycling
White River Watershed Council
Wicked Adventure Racing
Wild Turkey Federation
Wilderness Stewards
Wilderness Volunteers
Wildlife Society of Oregon
Willamette Industries
Wolf Run Irrigation Association
Wolftree, Inc
Women in Trees
World Forestry Center
Wy'east Book Shoppe & Art Gallery
Wy'east Kayak Rentals
Wy'east Nordic, Inc.
X-Dog Events
Zigzag Economic Development
    Corporation

*Thank you to the nearly 400
organizations and more than 1,400
individual volunteers.*

*With a list this long, it is possible to
miss someone. My sincere apologies to
anyone who is missing from the list.*

◁ Though not as well-known as skiing, dog sledding is popular on the mountain. This musher is enjoying a day with his dogs near Frog Lake.
△ The Palmer Snowfield attracts thousands of skiers for summer play.
▷▷ Moonlight illuminates a sulphur vent near Crater Rock.

△ Many miles of hiking trails are maintained on the mountain. At Alder Flat the trail winds through old-growth forest and lush undergrowth.
▷ Rhododendron almost seem out of place where only forest is expected. Here their delicate color accents Douglas-firs near Marco Creek.

A Sight So Nobly Grand

It was cool, but clear, that October day. Clear in the way Oregon fall days can be, where, if you're up high on a hill, you can stretch your gaze out like you would a cramped limb, gaze past the trees below you, beyond the river snaking into the distance, over the hills undulating like purple-blue waves to where the landscape blurs and the horizon curves with the shape of the earth.

Joel Palmer was indeed up high on a hill that day in October 1845. He had awakened that morning at his campsite in a meadow on the southwest flank of Mount Hood, a few miles from where Timberline Lodge now sits. After a quick breakfast, he and two companions continued their ascent of the mountain begun the day before. They headed up a grassy ravine until it became barren, then turned to snow and ice. Palmer's companions soon lagged behind but he forged on. Now, as the sun crept across the sky, Palmer found himself alone on the upper reaches of Oregon's highest mountain. The soles of his moccasins had worn clear through so that his bare feet gripped the ice of the glacier with each step.

After a time, he clambered up on a rock outcropping jutting up from the ice and snow to rest. Palmer was sitting on what would later be named Illumination Rock, roughly two thousand feet below the summit of Mount Hood. He was the first white man to climb this high on the mountain, but the feat was doubtless lost on him. He wasn't up here for glory or recognition. The purpose of his climb that day was purely practical: he was searching for a way through the Cascade Mountains for the eighty or so emigrants camped far below and to the east near the White River. Days earlier Palmer, who had departed his native Indiana six months before, leading a group of fifteen families, had joined up with Kentuckian Sam Barlow and his own group of nineteen Oregon Trail emigrants. Together, with their thirty wagons and dozens of horses and cattle, they were making the first-ever attempt by emigrants to reach the Willamette Valley from The Dalles by traveling around Mount

Hood rather than down the Columbia River, whose hazardous rapids had spelled the demise of many of their predecessors. But the emigrants were discovering that going overland posed as many perils as the river route. They had to cut a trail through the thick forest wide enough for their cattle and wagons—"horse canoes" as the Indians called them. Rivers gushed down from the glaciers of Mount Hood, making for hazardous crossings. Winter was rapidly approaching, and with it, the potential for storms that could prove deadly for anyone caught high in the mountains. And, most nerve-wracking of all for Palmer and Barlow, they were in uncharted territory, unable to see beyond the thickly timbered mountains a clear passage through the formidable range. And so Palmer found himself high on the snowy peak, looking out from that vantage point for a viable route to the emigrants' long-sought "Eden"—the Willamette Valley.

From Illumination Rock, Palmer climbed higher on the mountain, but did not reach the summit. He noted in his journal that he believed it possible to climb to the top. But the day was passing quickly and he needed to search the western mountains and ravines for a way through before beginning his descent and long hike back to camp. From somewhere above Illumination Rock, Palmer stood and let his eyes roam over the ridges and valleys below. His eyes kept returning to a "stream" which he was able to follow for several miles running southeast before turning west. This actually was the Salmon River. "A low gap seemed to connect this stream, or some other, heading in this high range, with the low bottoms immediately under the base of this peak," Palmer wrote in his journal. "I was of the opinion that a pass might be found between this peak and the first range of mountains, by digging down some of the gravel hills. . . ." Palmer had just discovered the route that the emigrants would use—a course that would pass through what is now Government Camp and down steep and rocky Laurel Hill. Palmer

◁ *This unnamed waterfall at Cast Creek was only discovered last year. With no trail leading to it, getting there is pure bushwhacking—actually walking in the stream for a few miles—but it's worth the effort!*

couldn't know it, but this route across the southwest flank of Mount Hood would not only take the emigrants safely to their destination, it would forever change man's relationship with the mountain.

Palmer descended the glacier, meeting up once again with his companions—one of whom was Sam Barlow, the man who would later build a road along the route Palmer had scouted. During the next weeks, Palmer and Barlow led their weary party across the route Palmer had seen from high on Mount Hood. The trip was treacherous; late fall storms forced the emigrants to leave their wagons and many belongings on the mountain in a makeshift fort and proceed to the Willamette Valley on foot through fog, rain, and snow. One of Barlow's starving horses died after eating rhododendron leaves—which the emigrants mistook for laurel—from the thick stands of the bushes covering the steep descent now known as Laurel Hill. But all of the emigrants made it, straggling in to the settlement of Oregon City over a span of several weeks. Palmer estimated that they had traveled a total of 1,960 miles from the Oregon Trail's jumping-off point at Independence, Missouri—the final trip from The Dalles around Mount Hood measuring 160 miles and, by most accounts, being the hardest of all. But he noted, "Actual measurement will vary these distances, most probably lessen them; and it is very certain, that by bridging the streams, the travel will be much shortened, by giving to it a more direct course, and upon ground equally favorable for a good road." His words would prove prophetic.

The story of Mount Hood begins, of course, long before Joel Palmer climbed it for a lookout. It begins long before the first Native Americans to inhabit the Columbia River Basin first laid eyes on it perhaps ten thousand years ago. Long, long before that (though a wink in geologic time), a little more than one million years ago, a small volcano located near the western base of present-day Mount Hood began erupting, forming the foundation of what would become Oregon's tallest mountain. The Sandy Glacier volcano, as it's known today, spewed basalt and andesite lavas from the earth, establishing itself into the landscape of existing low-lying volcanoes along the Cascade crest, and joined them in their ongoing battle with the Ice Age. During this era, known as

the Pleistocene, volcanoes along this crest built up through violent eruptions, only to be eroded away by the relentless advance of glaciers. It's impossible to know how big the Sandy Glacier volcano was, but it is the oldest of the modern High Cascade volcanoes, a swath of cordillera stretching from British Columbia to California. Basalt flows from that earlier volcano form today's Vista Ridge on Mount Hood's north side.

Glacial ice had likely eroded the Sandy Glacier volcano significantly by the time Mount Hood was born, between six hundred- and seven hundred thousand years ago. Mount Hood began forming practically on top of the earlier volcano, with alternating eruptions of ash and lava building it ever higher. As the Ice Age wore on through the centuries, eruptions of Mount Hood battled against glaciation. Its present height of 11,239 feet indicates that its eruptions were frequent enough and big enough to outlast the final throes of the Ice Age, which began its retreat twelve- to fifteen thousand years ago.

Other events occurred during the volatile prehistory of Mount Hood that contributed to its formation and the surrounding landscape. For hundreds of thousands of years, periodic debris flows of ice, rocks, mud, sand, and uprooted vegetation that began high on Mount Hood sped down its flanks and flowed far along the Sandy River and into the Hood River Valley. The most significant of these occurred between fifty- and one hundred thousand years ago when part of the northern face of Mount Hood collapsed. The resulting avalanche sent a catastrophic flow of rock and mud down the Hood River, burying the Hood River Valley to depths of more than 120 feet, creating a 100-foot-high dam across the Columbia River and continuing for two miles into Washington. The dam is long gone, but the north face of Mount Hood still bears the scar of that long-ago cataclysm. The volcanic remains left in the Hood River Valley would one day make it one of the richest tree fruit-growing regions on earth.

Native Americans began living along the Columbia River at the end of the Pleistocene era some ten thousand years ago. The mountain's ongoing rumblings and explosions became part of Native lore. Wy'East, as Mount Hood was known to the people who

lived around its base, was a fierce warrior who fought with Pa-Toe, his brother to the north (Mount Adams), for the affections of Beautiful Woman Mountain. She loved Wy'East, but flirted with Pa-Toe, and the brothers fought viciously, spewing lava and hurling rocks and fire at one another. The Great Spirit, Tyee Sahale, father of the warrior brothers, watched the ongoing battle with sadness. Loo-Wit, Beautiful Woman Mountain's guardian, tried to stop the destruction but she was old and weak. Eventually the Great Spirit rewarded her for her efforts by granting her wish for youth. She became the youngest of the Cascade Mountains, Mount St. Helens. Pa-Toe claimed Beautiful Woman Mountain as his own, but she was brokenhearted and slumped at Pa-Toe's feet, sinking into a deep slumber from which she never awoke. Pa-Toe, once tall and proud like Wy'East, was anguished and dropped his head in shame toward his lost love, now known as Sleeping Beauty Mountain southwest of Mount Adams.

Given Mount Hood's several eruptive phases over millennia, it's easy to see why the mountain was looked upon as a fierce and fire-spitting warrior by generations of Native Americans. About seventy-seven hundred years ago, a notable eruption occurred when a vent on the mountain's north side yawned open and began oozing molten lava and spitting basalt boulder "bombs." The lava flow extended three miles down the mountain before the eruption abruptly ceased. It's easy to imagine those long-ago residents—perhaps first startled by the vent's activity as they picked berries near the mountain's base high in the Hood River Valley—hurriedly returning to their villages by the Columbia River to tell of Wy'East's latest outburst. The lava flow can be seen today among the orchards of the Upper Hood River Valley, near Parkdale.

Much later, somewhere around eighteen hundred years ago, Mount Hood entered yet another eruptive phase. This time, vents on Mount Hood's southwest side spewed mostly ash, which poured down the Sandy, Salmon, and Zigzag Rivers. The last eruption on Mount Hood—at the tail end of this phase—has been precisely dated using tree rings from buried stumps to the winter of 1781–82. A powerful eruption originating at Crater Rock near the summit of

△ *Swirling snow seems to be trying to make its own funnel cloud above the Salmon River Canyon. The difference between blowing snow and clouds is sometimes nearly impossible to discern.*

the mountain sent lahars—volcanic mud flows—down the south-west slopes of Mount Hood, burying forests along the Sandy and Zigzag Rivers in as much as thirty feet of sticky ash and boulder-laden mud. This volcanic stew clogged the Sandy River all the way to its confluence with the Columbia, altering both rivers for decades.

The Sandy River was still flowing through silty volcanic sludge ten years later when Lieutenant William Broughton of the British Royal Navy paddled past it in a longboat. He had been sent to explore the Columbia River from its mouth by his commander, Captain George Vancouver, who hoped doing so would partly redeem him from being beaten to the discovery of the long-sought "Great River of the West" by American explorer Robert Gray. Broughton was a week into his river exploration when, on October 29, 1792, he rounded a bend near the confluence of the Willamette River and came upon an arresting view. In his log he wrote, "A very distant high snowy mountain now appeared rising beautifully conspicuous in the midst of an extensive tract of low, or moderately elevated, land. . . ." Broughton, the first white man to see the mountain, named it Mount Hood in honor of Lord Samuel Hood, admiral of the British Navy and the man who had commissioned Vancouver's voyage to the Northwest. Broughton continued up the Columbia River to the mouth of the gorge, not far past the Sandy River (which he named the Barings River). If he noticed its silted state and delta extending into the Columbia, he didn't remark about it in his log. Perhaps at that point he was preoccupied with Vancouver's ultimate order, which was to

△ *The Columbia River Gorge is a world-class site for windsurfing: the westward-flowing Columbia River is counterbalanced much of the year by east winds, creating ideal windsurfing conditions.*

determine the source of the Columbia. Before turning around and heading back downriver, Broughton surmised, incorrectly of course, that Mount Hood was the source of the Great River.

Some landmarks along the Lower Columbia retain Broughton's original names to this day, while others were renamed by later explorers and settlers. As for Mount Hood, despite subsequent misidentifications and attempts to rename the peak, Broughton's nod to Lord Hood stuck. Oregon's sentinel, its landmark and most recognizable icon, remains today named for a man from a distant country who never laid eyes on it.

It was thirteen years after Broughton saw and named Mount Hood from the west that explorers Lewis and Clark arrived in the Oregon territory from the east. They first noted the peak in their journals on October 18, 1805, with a simple sentence: ". . . Saw a mountain bearing S.W. Conocal form Covered with Snow . . ." A couple of days later, from an observation point next to the river near present-day Arlington, Lewis wrote, ". . . from this rapid the Conocil mountain is S.W. which the Indians inform me is not far to the left of the great falls [the once mighty Celilo Falls, submerged when The Dalles Dam was built in the 1950s] this I call the 'Timm' or falls mountain it is high and the top is covered with Snow . . ." The explorers continued to refer to the mountain as Timm or Falls mountain until they reached the Sandy River, when they finally recognized it as Broughton's Mount Hood.

Even more than two decades after the mountain's last eruption, the Sandy River still bore the signature of the upheaval. In

November 1805, the Corps of Discovery explored the wide delta then at the mouth of the river: "I arrived at the enterance of a river which appeared to Scatter over a Sand bar, the bottom of which I could See quite across and did not appear to be 4 Inches deep in any part; I attempted to wade this Stream and to my astonishment found the bottom a quick Sand, and impassable . . ." Clark wrote. An additional notation reads, ". . . This river throws out emence quantitys of sand and is very shallow, the narrowest part 200 yards wide . . ." The explorers named it the Quicksand River, a designation which stuck until the middle of the nineteenth century when it began appearing on maps as the abbreviated Sandy River.

In the decades after Lewis and Clark's expedition, Mount Hood was seen and remarked upon by prospectors, traders, missionaries, fur trappers, and scientists who made their way to the Oregon territory by land from the north and the east, and by sea from the west. David Douglas, the famed Scottish botanist for whom the Douglas-fir tree is named, proclaimed Mount Hood unclimbable when he first saw the mountain in 1825: "In June I was within a few miles of Mount Hood. its appearance presented barriers that could not be surmounted by any person to reach the summit."

Captain Nathaniel Wyeth, a New Englander, journeyed to the Oregon territory in 1832 with the dream of establishing a trading empire. He spotted Mount Hood on October 20 from a boat on the Columbia in eastern Oregon, remarking in his journal on "a large snowy mountain, southwest by west, called by the French 'Montague de Neige.'" A few days later, he wrote, "We passed the high mountain covered with snow . . . It is on the left of the river and is a more stupendous pile than any of the Rocky Mountains."

Trappers came to the region throughout the early decades of the 1800s in search of beaver for the ladies' hats then popular in East Coast cities. From the few existing writings of these early explorers, it's clear Mount Hood was seen not only as an icon of the territory, but was used for such practical purposes as measuring distances. It was the trappers and other early explorers of the Oregon territory who lured the first of the Oregon Trail emigrants to head west, and in 1842, the first wagon train made it to the Willamette Valley. The next year more than nine hundred emi-grants made the trek. After months of travel, emigrants first saw Mount Hood from the Blue Mountains and it became a potent symbol of the end of their journey. But they soon discovered that the mountain, ever more striking a vision as they got nearer, proved to be the final—and ultimate—obstacle to their destination. Getting beyond it to the Willamette Valley meant descending the treacherous Columbia River at its northern foot. And so Mount Hood was looked upon with trepidation by early settlers.

By the time Joel Palmer and Sam Barlow got to The Dalles in 1845, they were part of some three thousand emigrants who arrived that year. Many were stuck in The Dalles in a bottle-neck, forced to wait for the two riverboat captains that guided emigrants—for a tidy sum—down the river. The time was ripe to find an alternate route to Oregon City, and that's exactly what Palmer and Barlow did.

Barlow knew the value of establishing an alternative to the river passage, and had scarcely rested from his overland journey and last arduous push around Mount Hood when he applied to the terri-torial government for a charter to build a toll road along the route. He and a crew of forty men began work on the road as soon as weather permitted in the spring of 1846. They used axes, saws, and fire to clear the route. Wagon trains began using the primitive road that year (records show that 145 wagons passed through during the toll road's inaugural season) but it wasn't completed until 1848. Initially, a tollhouse was set up on the east side of the route, near Wamic, with Barlow charging the relatively exorbitant sum of $5 per wagon for passage. Later the toll station was moved to the west side, where it was set in several locations before finally being placed just east of present-day Rhododendron.

The Barlow Road soon became the route of choice for emi-grants, but it still presented perhaps the greatest hardships the overland travelers had experienced on their entire journey across the continent. The road was cut crudely across the ridges and ravines of Mount Hood's waist, often right over huge rocks or roughly-cut tree stumps that posed hazards for wagons. Muddy conditions caused the road to become deeply rutted so that wagon wheels often sank precariously on one side or the other.

And the most perilous part of all lay, cruelly, near the very end: Laurel Hill. The only way off this "shelf" of the mountain was straight down the steep, rocky terrain. The road here was nothing more than a chute—or several of them—that emigrants had to descend at great risk to their lives and belongings. The favored method of navigating the chutes was to cut down huge trees and tie them to the wagons as anchors, and then to tie the wagons to enormous trees at the sides of the chutes and winch them slowly down the precipice. Emigrant Absolom Harden on September 20, 1847, wrote of the hill simply: "This is the worse hill on the road from the States to Oregon." Things were no better two decades later when S. B. Eakin wrote about his trip down Laurel Hill on August 19, 1866: "Can you imagine what the mountain is like. It is one mile long and that steep that we keep the hind wheels locked, and the mules holding back their best all the time. Heavy timber and quick turns to make with four mules. While descending this hill, or mountain, Grandma was sitting in the back seat of the buggy; she could not hold herself in but fell forward and struck the ground head first. She was hurt but little by the fall. We then put her in my wagon in the bottom of the box."

△ *First light bathes white bark pine krummholz high along the Texas Trails at Mount Hood Meadows. Though the word* Krummholz *has several uses, one is to refer to the matlike surface of pine remnants on exposed ridges above tree line.*

In 1849, the Barlow Road gained notoriety when the Army sent 250 tons of supplies from Fort Leavenworth, Kansas, to outfit Oregon forts, and a train of more than 400 wagons and 1,700 mules was routed over the mountain road. The caravan camped near the summit, in a spot known thereafter as the Government Camp. Before they even confronted the perils of Laurel Hill, the Army had to abandon 45 wagons after dozens of mules died from starvation.

The construction of the Barlow Road, despite its primitive nature, ushered in a new era on Mount Hood. Prior to it, only animal and Indian trails existed—many of them one and the same. For millennia, a primordial silence had permeated the mountain, interrupted only by the sounds of nature—wind, rain, rock slides, gushing rivers, bird calls—and, for the last few thousand years,

the occasional footsteps of Native Americans. Suddenly, in a few years time, Mount Hood's virgin landscapes were touched by more humans than at any time in its 700,000-year existence. The mountain's very nature changed from that of daunting obstacle to conquerable object. Mankind had begun to make his indelible mark on the mountain.

Indeed, it didn't take long for adventurous-minded settlers, once they'd made it around Mount Hood out of necessity, to look upon the mountain as a source of recreation and pleasure. The first authenticated climb to the summit took place in July 1857 when a party of four Portlanders—including Henry Pittock, founder of the *Oregonian*—planted a flag at the summit. A member of the group, Reverend T. A. Wood, wrote about the July 11, 1857, climb: "At 3 o'clock we reached the summit of Mount Hood. Never in

all my life have I seen a grander or more impressive sight . . . To the east we could trace the Columbia River, apparently, as far as Fort Walla Walla. We could see the Blue Mountains and the rolling prairies. To the north there were three snow-capped mountain peaks—St. Helens, Rainier and Adams. To the northwest we saw two lakes which have never been explored, and which have probably never been visited by a white man [probably Bull Run and Lost Lakes] . . . To the westward we could see Portland . . . We saw a smoke at Oregon City which we decided came from a foundry there. With our glasses we could see a cluster of houses marking the site of Salem. To the south we could see several snow-capped peaks. We counted five lakes of various sizes, shining like looking glasses. To the east rose . . . the Blue Mountains while far to the west was the softened outline of the Coast range. Above us the

sky was a deep Prussian blue. The north side of the mountain falls off almost perpendicularly." A climber standing on the summit today sees a strikingly similar panorama.

Climbing Mount Hood led to other pursuits on the mountain—some recreational, others not. In the patriotic post–Civil War 1870s, an idea was hatched to illuminate the upper part of Mount Hood for the Fourth of July. Years went by before a viable plan came about to attempt it, but in 1887, a group of seven men set out from Portland with one hundred pounds of "red fire," highly flammable lycopodium powder. On the morning of the Fourth, they headed up from their camp above timberline. Snow had been heavy that year, and as the day wore on, they realized they would not reach the summit, as planned. By afternoon, they'd settled on a place below a jutting rock formation to carry

out their scheme. The rock formation was the same one Joel Palmer had clambered up for a rest some forty years before. That night, the explosives were ignited at 11:30 P.M. For fifty-eight seconds, the upper reaches of Mount Hood were bathed in red light, an unforgettable sight seen up and down the Willamette Valley. Reports of the successful illumination of Mount Hood appeared in newspapers around the country and even in Europe, and Illumination Rock had its name.

For the first few decades after settlers began to arrive in Oregon, attention on Mount Hood was focused on the south side, with its access from Portland via the Barlow Road. But by the 1880s, the Hood River Valley below the mountain's north face was gaining prominence. In 1882 the Oregon Rail & Navigation Company laid tracks through the gorge, suddenly making the previously isolated Hood River Valley an easy train ride from Portland. From the Hood River depot, a road led halfway up the Hood River Valley to near the base of the mountain. In 1884, settlers built a rough road from that midway point through thick forest to near timberline where a tent camp was established at the six-thousand-foot level, just below Eliot Glacier. The camp attracted adventurous summer tourists from as far away as the Willamette Valley and beyond.

In 1889, two Portlanders who had become enamored of the camp bought the road to it, improved it, and soon began constructing a timber lodge on a rock promontory near where the tent camp had been. Giant firs felled miles below were hauled up to the building site, and the rough-hewn timber logs were bolted together one by one. Rock blasted from nearby cliffs was used to build two great fireplaces. When the lodge was completed, the entire structure was anchored to the rock by heavy steel cables.

The Cloud Cap Inn opened in 1889 as the first alpine resort in the West. Many people—even those involved in the project— worried that the inn would not be able to withstand the howling winds and heavy snows that pummel Mount Hood during winter. During a lull in storms in February 1890, two Hood River Valley residents set out on cross-country skis to find out the fate of the lodge. When they arrived two days later, they found that snow had drifted inside, but otherwise the lodge was in fine shape.

Increased public use of forest lands led to the creation of the Cascade Range Forest Reserve in 1893. The designation came a year after the Bull Run Reserve west of Mount Hood had been established and made off-limits to the public in order to safeguard Portland's water supply. (The area had earlier been dubbed Bull Run by emigrants whose cattle had broken free while rounding the mountain and headed to this isolated western flank of the mountain.) The sprawling Cascade Range Forest Reserve was first administered by the General Land Office (now the Bureau of Land Management) and was initially part of the Interior Department, but was transferred to the Forest Service bureau within the Department of Agriculture in 1905. In 1908 the Cascade Range Forest Reserve, which covered much of the Oregon Cascades, was divided up into several National Forests; the northern portion, including Mount Hood and the Bull Run Reserve, was called the Oregon National Forest. In 1924, the name was changed to the Mount Hood National Forest. It originally included more than 1.7 million acres, extending from the Columbia River south to Mount Jefferson. (The southern portion later became part of the Willamette National Forest.) The creation of the Cascade Range Forest Reserve, at a time when a national debate raged about forest lands and public versus private ownership of them, ensured that Mount Hood and its surrounding lands would forever remain in the public domain—an auspicious foresight not universally favored at the time.

The popularity of Mount Hood as a recreation destination was cemented the year after the Cascade Range Forest Reserve was established when an ad was placed in the *Oregonian* on June 12, 1894, which read: "To Mountain Climbers and Lovers of Nature . . . It has been decided to meet on the summit of Mt. Hood on the 19th of next month . . ." Response to the ad was overwhelming: on July 18, more than three hundred people were camped on the southern flank of the mountain and the next day 193 men and women climbed to the summit. Thus, the Mazamas were born, becoming the first mountaineering society in the West. Their goals were to foster mountain leadership, safety, conservation, and climbing education. Membership was limited to those who had reached the summit of Mount Hood, or another glaciered peak. Other

▷ *The palette of fall colors along the East Fork of the Hood River at Toll Bridge Park is varied enough to keep any painter happy.*

mountain-oriented organizations followed: the Snowshoe Club, an exclusive group of Portland mountain-lovers who built their own lodge near the Cloud Cap Inn; the Triangle Club, a YMCA-affiliated group of climbers; and some time later, the Wy'east Climbers, the Alpine Club, the Crag Rats, and—from necessity—Portland Mountain Rescue.

After the formation of the Mazamas—and perhaps partly because of them—climbing, hiking, skiing, and general outings on Mount Hood grew increasingly popular during the early 1900s. Climbing routes on the south and north sides of the peak became well established. The most popular south-side route started at Government Camp, headed through forestland to timberline, up Palmer Glacier to the Hog's Back and on to the summit. On the north side, climbers began at Cloud Cap, headed up Cooper Spur and continued on above Eliot Glacier to the summit. At the end of the 1800s, a few hundred people a year stood atop Mount Hood. By the 1920s, well over twice that signed the summit log annually.

In 1921, the Hood River Post of the American Legion began hosting annual climbs of the north side each July that became legendary for their size—within a few years nearly 200 people were participating. Not to be outdone, the Mazamas led equally popular climbs up the south side. In 1922, 102 climbers from the Legion outing mingled with 70 Mazamas at the summit; mountain-climbing traffic jams had officially begun.

Hiking and camping in the vast wilderness areas below timberline also grew popular as increasing numbers of Oregonians with more modest goals than reaching the summit flocked to Mount Hood. In the hurried years around the turn of the twentieth century, as the Industrial Revolution ground on, people were realizing the benefits of nature. Around this time, John Muir wrote: "Thousands of tired, nerve-shaken, over-civilized people are beginning to find out that going to the mountains is going home; that wilderness is a necessity." In deference to this growing popular sentiment, the Forest Service began expanding its network

△ *Nestled beneath the mountain, Trillium Lake draws a solitary kayaker to its serene beauty. To guard the tranquillity, no motors are allowed on the lake.*

of trails in Mount Hood's wilderness. Hiking clubs often teamed up with the Forest Service to help build trails, sometimes seeking financial help from like-minded philanthropists. A campaign by the Mazamas in the early 1920s for a trail to Paradise Park from the old Barlow Road led to sponsorship by Portland lumber baron Simon Benson. Soon after, plans were hatched for a trail to encircle Mount Hood at around the six-thousand-foot level. Within a few years, trail crews—many part of Franklin Delano Roosevelt's Depression-era Civilian Conservation Corps— were working on sections of what would eventually become the forty-mile Timberline Trail. The CCC also made improvements to the long-used Tilly Jane Trail on the mountain's north slope and to the popular campground at Lost Lake.

The popularity of Mount Hood as a recreation and sight-seeing destination in the early 1900s also led to growing demand for a road encircling the mountain. Improvements to the Barlow Road in the early 1900s by its final private owner, Henry Wemme, made it easier for Portlanders to reach the mountain. Similarly, by 1915 the Columbia River Highway provided a beautiful drive up the Gorge, where motorists could then proceed high into the Hood River Valley on a well-maintained road. Only a twenty-three-mile stretch between the upper Hood River Valley and Government Camp remained roadless. After a scouting party mapped a route to connect the north and south sides, road construction began in 1919. It took six years to complete, but the resulting Mount Hood Loop Highway was an instant success, attracting motorists from around the region. Quaint inns and lodges located along the route provided a range of accommodations.

Most of the road was closed in winter due to snow, but in 1926 the state highway department began plowing during the winter from Sandy to Government Camp. Winter automobile access contributed much to the popularity of skiing on the mountain's south side. In 1927, a lighted toboggan slide and ski area opened near Government Camp, with enough parking for 750 cars. In the next few years, ski

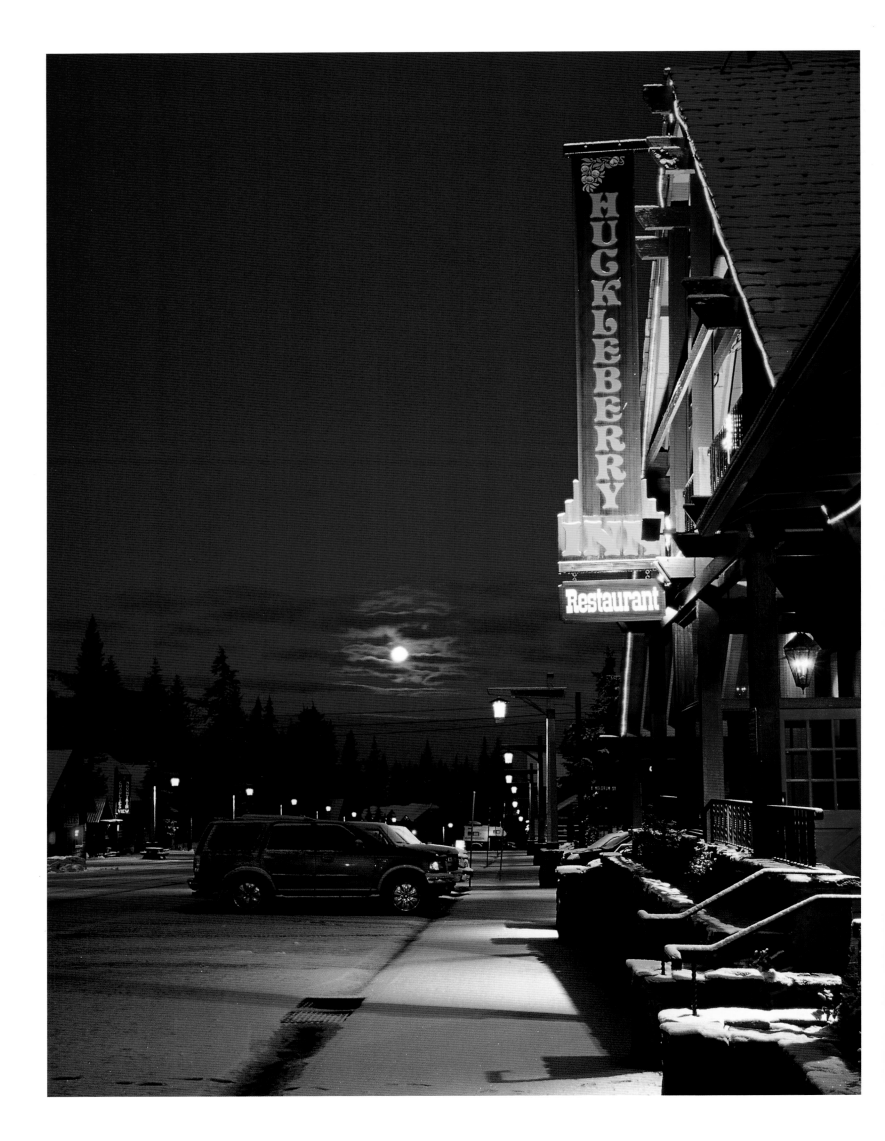

runs on Multorpor Mountain were cut, and ski races and other events were held there and on other primitive ski runs nearby.

By the 1930s the Northwest was in the throes of the Depression. The Cloud Cap Inn had closed years before due to financial problems. Plans to revamp and enlarge the inn had surfaced in fits and starts for several years, finally dying out completely with the crash of the stock market. But the idea of a large lodge, accessible to all, on the flanks of Mount Hood remained dear to many Portland movers and shakers. When one of those men, Emerson Griffith, was appointed to head the Works Progress Administration in Oregon, the dream of building such a lodge suddenly became a reality. The Forest Service granted use of land at timberline above Government Camp—where most of the skiing and winter recreation was now taking place, due to its proximity to Portland—and agreed to sign on to the project as a sponsor. Seeing that the project would provide work for a variety of people—laborers as well as artists and craftspeople—and provide recreation and scenic preservation, the WPA headquarters in Washington, D.C., readily approved the project in 1935.

Construction of Timberline Lodge—whose unique architectural style spawned a new term, Cascadian—began in the spring of 1936 and became, arguably, the most impressive WPA project in the country, employing nearly five hundred people at its height. The interior was designed around three main themes: the pioneer experience, Indian symbols and legends, and native flora and fauna. Craftsmen created massive carvings along these themes while artists made everything from glass and tile mosaics to paintings for decorating the forty-eight rooms. A team of Portland women made more than one hundred hooked rugs, hand-sewn and appliquéd curtains, and wove nearly one thousand yards of drapery and furniture fabric. Ironworkers fashioned more than one hundred and eighty unique pieces, ranging from gates to hinges. More than eight hundred pieces of furniture were designed and handmade for the lodge. Even dozens of spun copper ashtrays were made by hand. Laborers hauled four hundred tons of stone from the slopes of Mount Hood to construct the ninety-two-foot-high chimney rising through the middle of the main lobby. Timberline Lodge was dedicated by President Roosevelt in September 1937, with final completion a few months later. In 1939, the Magic Mile opened, then the longest ski chairlift in the United States.

In many ways, the construction of Timberline Lodge ushered in the modern era on Mount Hood. It was the first time large numbers of people could stay, sheltered inside in comfort, high up on the mountain year-round. In a mere ninety years—a single, if generous, lifetime—since Joel Palmer had scouted a route across it, skiers, outdoor enthusiasts, and simply tourists were flocking to Mount Hood in every season. Near the time Timberline Lodge was completed, Portland newspaperman and Mount Hood historian Fred McNeil wrote: "Highways and trails have opened to the easy access of thousands. Some of the old-timers see these changes with regret. They would keep the peak for those who have the strength and courage to face the difficulties attending its approach. But Mount Hood has room for all, the weak with the strong, and there are plenty of places about the peak which will be attained, as before, only by those who take the risks to get there."

In the nearly seventy years since the construction of Timberline Lodge, man's presence on Mount Hood has grown exponentially. The 1950s brought the nationwide skiing boom to the slopes of the mountain in earnest. Timberline Lodge, after several years of decline beginning during World War II, underwent a revival under the management of Richard Kohnstamm, who restored its earlier glory and initiated many improvements over the next decades. With its location on Palmer Glacier, Timberline enjoys the distinction of being the only U.S. ski area open year-round. In recent years it's become a favorite venue for summer snowboard and ski camps, and serves as a summer training site for the U.S. Ski Team. On the mountain's north side, Cooper Spur Ski Area became popular with Hood River Valley residents after World War II. In 1968, to the list of Mount Hood's four ski areas was added Mt. Hood Meadows, located farther to the east than any of the others in order to take advantage of the drier conditions on that side of the mountain. That year, the state highway department began plowing the Mount Hood Loop Highway in its entirety year-round, assuring continual access to all the mountain's winter recreation sites.

Along with winter sports, Mount Hood's popularity for other recreation has exploded during the past few decades. Hundreds of

◁ *A 4:00 A.M. moonset lights the snow-dusted streets of Government Camp.*

31

miles of trails provide a playground for mountain bikers, hikers, and horseback riders. The number of campers on the mountain, using both designated areas and remote wilderness, grows annually. The Mount Hood National Forest, now encompassing nearly 1.1 million acres, hosts more than four million visitors every year—nearly three times as many as visit any other federal forest in Oregon. Five designated wilderness areas, plus part of a sixth—the Hatfield, Mount Hood, Salmon-Huckleberry, Badger Creek, Bull-of-the-Woods, and Mount Jefferson—encompass 189,000 acres. Even these primitive areas without roads see nearly 140,000 visitors annually. And then, there's climbing. Mount Hood is now the most-climbed glaciered peak in the United States (second in the world only to Japan's Mount Fuji) with more than 10,000 people each year attempting its summit. And, of course, Mount Hood is muse and mentor for many who seek its slopes for artistic or spiritual reasons or, simply, solitude.

And where, in the story of Mount Hood, are some of its early characters? Portions of the Barlow Road are today popular hiking trails maintained by the U.S. Forest Service. Wagon ruts can still be seen in places, and the infamous chutes are still visible not far from where Highway 26 winds up Laurel Hill. If you look closely, you can still see notches on trees where wagons were winched down the precipice. Government Camp, that long-ago rest stop for an Army caravan, has undergone a revival in recent years. An urban renewal project begun in the late 1980s has turned the once-dilapidated community into a quaint tourist hub. A new condominium development promises to bring crowds year-round to the mountain's only destination resort. The Cloud Cap Inn, which many doubted could withstand one winter on Mount Hood, has now stood for 116 of them. The Crag Rats, a renowned Hood River–based mountain rescue organization established in the 1920s, maintain the lodge and use it as their base for training and rescues. In 1974, Cloud Cap was placed on Oregon's Registry of Historic Places. The Mount Hood Loop Highway is now a designated State Scenic Byway. Timberline Lodge continues to remain a successful and historic destination—truly, a living museum.

Some of the actual characters who helped forge man's bond with Mount Hood are indelibly part of the mountain, brought to life every day as their lyrical names—most associated with the early days in Portland, the Hood River Valley, or the mountain itself—roll off our tongues: Eliot Glacier, Cooper Spur, Coalman Glacier, Langille Glacier, Newton Clark Glacier, Barrett Spur. Other names, equally lyrical, conjure their descriptive origins: Zigzag Glacier (named after Joel Palmer's description of descending the deep ravine near Timberline on his 1845 scouting mission—and, appropriately, the very glacier he ascended with worn-out moccasins), Elk Cove, Eden Park, Heather Canyon, Cairn Basin, Castle Crags, Cathedral Ridge. Mount Hood's eleven glaciers continue to etch their story onto the mountain's many faces. As for Wy'East's periodic outbursts, they will be seen again. Mount Hood is very much alive—as any climber knows who's witnessed the vents and fumaroles near the summit exhaling its sulfur-smelling breath. Frequent earthquake swarms emanating from deep within the mountain could portend a future eruption—an event geologists don't question will take place, only when.

Joel Palmer couldn't possibly have foreseen how Mount Hood—which, shortly before his historic climb, he described as "a sight so nobly grand"—would be shaped by the people of Oregon, or how so many people would be shaped by Mount Hood. "Our mountain," as Oregonians fondly call it, has a mesmerizing effect on its witnesses. Naturalist Dallas Lore Sharp, visiting Oregon around 1910, fell under its spell: "There are loftier mountains," he wrote, "Rainier and Adams are loftier; there are peaks that fill with awe and that strike with terror, while Hood only fills the soul with exultation, with the joy of beauty, of completeness and perfection. . . . Its greatness is not physical, not height nor power; but form rather, and spirit, and position. Mount Hood from Portland is one of the perfect things in the world. I look down from Council Crest upon the growing city and see the present moment of my country hurried, crowded, headlong. Then I lift my eyes to Hood, serene and soaring in the far-off Heaven, and lo! A vision of the future! Not the Mountain that was God, but a summit that is song."

That was a century ago, but it could have been yesterday. May we steward Mount Hood so that those words ring true a century from now, so that our children's grandchildren can hear the song.

▷ *Purple-hued lupine, interspersed with occasional bright red paintbrush, carpet an alpine meadow at Elk Cove.*

◁ On their first backpacking trip ever, students from Springwater Trail
High School in Gresham enjoy the view from the Dollar Lake campsite.
△ Fireweed seedpods glisten in afternoon sun near McGee Creek. The
plant is one of the first to move into cleared or burned-off woodlands.
▷▷ At dawn, the waters of Eliot Creek evoke feelings of drama and
power, peace and tranquillity. Eliot Creek, which starts as meltwater
from Eliot Glacier, flows into the Middle Fork of the Hood River.

△ Salmon may migrate several thousand miles into the salty waters of
the sea from the time they leave the freshwater rivers as juveniles until
they return as adults. Here, salmon return to spawn in Eagle Creek.
▷ A single avalanche lily brightens Wy'east Basin. As soon as the snow
melts, avalanche lilies carpet the forest floor with their delicate blossoms.

◁ Receding snow reveals rocky terrain near the Coe Glacier. On Mount Hood's north side, the Coe is the mountain's most difficult ice climb.
△ Winter blankets the White River at the White River Sno-Park.

△ Climbers atop a 350-foot spire called Monkey Face at Smith Rock State Park take in a view of Mount Hood. The park embraces several thousand climbs, as well as miles of hiking and mountain biking trails.

△ The West Fork of the Hood River reveals columns of basalt rock, the result of cooled basaltic lava. Basaltic lava can flow quickly, moving several miles from a vent. Basalt is earth's most common type of rock. ▷▷ A springtime aerial of the North Face of Mount Hood reveals Mount Jefferson on the distant horizon.

△ Timberline Trail, a forty-mile path that circles Mount Hood, passes by a waterfall decorated with lupine, paintbrush, and cow parsnip.
▷ A weathered pine remnant graces a windy ridge at McNeil Point.

◁ Purple lupine softens the harsh rock edges in the boulder-strewn Cairn Basin, near Vista Ridge on the remote northwest side of the mountain. △ The Pacific Crest Trail overlooks the Bull Run Reservoir. Protected since 1892 when President Benjamin Harrison established the Bull Run Reserve, the waters of the Bull Run provide more than 25 percent of Oregon's drinking water. Portland residents first took delivery of water from the Bull Run watershed in 1895.

△ Built by the Civilian Conservation Corps in 1934, this wooden shelter
at Elk Meadows is one of the last such shelters on the Timberline Trail.
▷ A sun-bleached white bark pine stands alone at Elk Cove.

◁ The setting sun backlights blooming bear grass near Vista Ridge.
△ Waterfalls plunge from cliffs across the Sandy River Canyon. Seasonal
and permanent waterfalls abound in the Mount Hood National Forest.

△ An early morning sunburst lights up the rim of the Devils Kitchen Headwall near the summit of Mount Hood. The headwall is near the Steel Cliffs, to the east of the Hogsback, a popular climbing route that leads to the pinnacle of the mountain.

△ Warm light bathes the Sandy River. The 2,650-mile Pacific Crest Trail crosses here as it wends its way from the Mexican border to Canada. ▷▷ The cascading waters of Ramona Falls make it a popular destination for day trips. The volume of water is actually less than one might expect, but this waterfall fans out to a wide base, creating a stunning display.

◁ Cottonwood and golden larch brighten the East Fork of Hood River.
△ A fisherman finds tranquillity in the Salmon River's pristine waters.
There are many ways in addition to fishing to earn such solitude: back-
packing, kayaking, and camping, to name just a few.

△ Climbers on the South Side route to the summit of Mount Hood traverse the Hogsback. More than ten thousand climbers register to climb to Hood's 11,239-foot peak each year.

△ Star trails overhead and a glowing campfire near Cloud Cap Inn show
why so many enjoy camping in the Mount Hood National Forest. With
no distracting city lights, the heavens seem close enough to touch.

△ Wildflowers provide a lush carpet in a meadow at Paradise Park, picking up and repeating the pastel colors on the mountain above at day's end.
▷ A hiker enjoys the view along the historic Barlow Road trail.

◁ Snow and ice encase the Sahalie Falls, creating a winter wonderland.
△ A 1930s Works Progress Administration (WPA) project, Timberline Lodge was constructed at the 6,600-foot level on Mount Hood. The lodge was dedicated in 1937 by President Franklin D. Roosevelt.

△ The pine tree is the official symbol of the U.S. Forest Service. The Forest Service began its management of the national forests in 1905.
▷ Recreationists going to Timothy and Olallie Lakes often stop by the Clackamas Lake Historic Ranger Station near Timothy Lake. The ranger station offers information as well as tours of the historic facility.
▷▷ Water from the Laurance Lake settling pond helps irrigate the upper Hood River Valley. The pond is the site of an annual kids fishing derby.

△ A hiker enjoys a view of Reid Glacier from the Yocum Ridge Trail.
▷ A trail winds behind the Tamanawas Falls, enabling one to feel the
power and mist. The falls' hundred-foot drop can be reached by a hike
of just a couple of miles off Highway 35 on Mount Hood's east side.

◁ Pear blossoms frame Mount Hood in the Hood River Valley. Hood
River County is the number one pear-growing county in the nation.
△ Kerosene smudge pots protect a pear crop from freezing temperatures.

△ The main branch of the Hood River flows with white-water swift-
ness near Apple Valley Country Store. Three major forks combine to
make up the mainstream Hood River.

△ Wintery winds swirl over the Barrett Spur, 7,850 feet in elevation.
▷▷ Brilliant vine maples contrast the dark gray lava rock in the sprawling expanse of the Lava Beds Geologic Area near Parkdale. The area's eruptive history dates from 7,500 years to just 250 years ago.

△ Oaks frame the confluence of the West and Middle Forks of the Hood River. Originating on Mount Hood, the Hood River merges with the Columbia twenty-two miles upstream of the Bonneville Dam.

△ Kingsley Reservoir is a popular site for a number of recreational activities, including mountain biking, fishing, and swimming. One event, the Mountain Man Off-Road Festival, includes both a Triathlon and a Half Marathon; both competitions begin and end at the Kingsley Reservoir.

△ Fall colors along Forest Service Road 48 on the way to Bonney Butte include greens and golds along with the vibrant red of vine maple, all backdropped by the ever-looming snow-covered peak of Mount Hood.
▷ Paintbrush scatters its brilliance at Mount Hood Meadows.

◁ Clark Creek flows through Heather Canyon. Towering above the canyon, Mount Hood sets off the rushing creek and the steep canyon walls.
△ The Salmon River's headwaters rise near Timberline Lodge.

△ The brilliant gold of larch trees near the Badger Creek Wilderness frame a mountain "hooded" by a lenticular cloud. The Badger Creek Wilderness encompasses some fifty-five miles of trails, including the Badger Creek National Recreation Trail, which stretches the length of the creek in the wilderness, a distance of nearly twelve miles.

△ Fall colors, clouds, and mist soften the lines of both the actual Mount Hood and its reflection in Lost Lake, a deep, clear, freshwater lake covering almost three hundred surface acres.

△ Smoke from a forest fire intensifies a sunset view of Mount St. Helens. The May 18, 1980, eruption of Mount St. Helens blew some 1,300 feet off the top of the mountain, bringing its present elevation to 8,364 feet.

△ A spotlight of sun lights up a trillium near Summit Prairie Meadows.
▷▷ Towering seracs show the power inherent in Eliot Glacier. Eliot is
one of eleven glaciers that cling to the upper reaches of Mount Hood.

◁ Crevasses, deep fissures in the glacier ice, form patterns at Eliot Glacier.
△ Crag Rats, an elite search and rescue group, practice climbing out of a
crevasse. The Crag Rats, the nation's oldest mountain search and rescue
organization, are charter members of the Mountain Rescue Association.

△ A replica of England's famous Stonehenge, the pillars of Stonehenge, near Maryhill Museum on the Washington side of the Columbia River, frame Mount Hood at sunset. The first monument constructed in our nation in memory of those who died in World War I, the Stonehenge at Maryhill was built by Sam Hill (1857–1931).

△ A grouse's natural camouflage enables it to blend quite nicely with the rocky terrain near the Langille Crags, which rise just east of the Langille Glacier. The crags and the glacier were named for the family that first operated Cloud Cap Inn in the 1890s.

△ Open fairways and hilly terrain—and, of course, views of Mount Hood—are all hallmarks of the Persimmon Country Club in Gresham. Not as well-known is the fact that in places on the well-kept grounds three other mountains are visible: Mounts St. Helens, Jefferson, and Adams.

△ The stern-wheeler *Columbia Gorge* carries swimmers to Hood River for the annual Roy Webster Columbia River Cross Channel Swim. The stern-wheeler runs day cruises on the Willamette and the Columbia.

△ Crag Rats ascend the Snow Dome in search of a missing climber. Founded in 1926, the all-volunteer Crag Rats are among the first to respond to an emergency on the mountain, as well as in the Columbia River Gorge and throughout the surrounding area.

△ Evening light creates a romantic setting at the historic Cloud Cap Inn, mountain headquarters for the Crag Rats search and rescue organization. Built in 1889 at the 6,000-foot elevation on the northeast shoulder of Mount Hood, Cloud Cap averages sixty *feet* of snow each winter.

△ A climber celebrates success in reaching the summit of Mount Hood.
▷ A fisherman enjoys the solitude of Mirror Lake. The area around the
lake is also great for hiking, especially when fall colors are at their peak.
▷▷ A skier jumps over a corniced ridge on the Palmer Glacier.

◁ Timberline Lodge is the site for numerous mountain- and snow-related activities—among them summer snowboarding competitions.
△ Snowshoers cross a bridge over Clark Creek.

△ A Forest Service crew replaces a washed-out bridge spanning the Sandy River. The name is a shortened form of what Lewis and Clark called it— the Quicksand River—after finding the mouth of the river impassable because its bottom was covered with quicksand.

△ A cloudy "sea" near Cathedral Ridge stretches to the horizon. At times the clouds around the mountain, as well as the shapes they assume, are as interesting as the mountain itself.

△ A vine maple leaf rests on early fall snow near Laurance Lake. Vine maple is one of Oregon's most colorful trees, turning brilliant red in fall. ▷ A pine snag frames a fiery winter sunset over Timberline Lodge. ▷▷ From the Pittock Mansion at dawn, the silhouette of Mount Hood looms beyond the lights of the city of Portland.

◁ Paintbrush and mountain heather carpet the ground at Wy'east Basin.
△ A snow bridge forms a tunnel over the Zigzag River. Obviously, care
is needed: what looks like a solid place to stand may not be safe at all.

△ A Japanese climber unwraps sushi to share with his friends on the summit of Mount Hood. People come from all over the world to enjoy the view, and the camaraderie, at the top of the world, Oregon-style.

△ An elk herd of between two- and three thousand ranges in the Mount Hood National Forest. Roosevelt elk usually roam west of the Cascades; Rocky Mountain elk, to the east. Roosevelt elk are larger and darker than Rocky Mountain elk; their antlers, shorter and heavier. The two varieties often mix to form the Mount Hood herd.

△ A collage of fall colors brightens the forest near Dog River Trail.
▷ Scattered across the ground, brilliant red vine maple leaves partner with
tree roots to create an intricate design at the Sherwood Campground.
▷▷ Little Crater Lake's clear waters come from a natural artesian spring.
Less than one hundred feet across, the lake is forty-five feet deep.

◁ Condos at Collins Lake Resort signal development at Government
Camp. In fall 1849, mounted riflemen headed to Oregon City over the
Barlow Road. Bad weather forced them to abandon a number of cavalry
wagons beside the trail, thus inspiring the name *Government Camp*.
△ A stone shelter gives comfort for skiers and climbers at Cooper Spur.
▷▷ Sunlight bursts through morning fog near Tilly Jane Campground.

△ Snow turns a boulder field into a winter moonscape in the White River basin. The glacier-fed White River flows off the east side of Mount Hood.
▷ A thunderhead above the mountain signals an approaching storm.
▷▷ On a calm spring evening, lights from the Hood River/White Salmon Interstate Bridge are reflected in the Columbia River.

△ With a seventy-inch wingspan and a thirty-eight-inch length, a great blue heron *(Ardea herodias)* patiently waits for fish at Eagle Creek. Its grey-blue coloring, long legs, and large bill are also distinguishing features.
▷ Children (without wings) fly down the alpine slide at Ski Bowl.

◁ An infant's tombstone at the Pioneer Cemetery near Summit Prairie
Meadows points out the fragility of life in Oregon Territory in the 1800s.
△ Andesite outcroppings above 15 Mile Creek evoke images of other-
worldly stone creatures just waiting to be brought to life.

△ Since 1992, the number of wineries in Oregon has more than tripled, making the growing of wine grapes, such as these at Carabella Vineyard in Willamette Valley, a major segment of the state's agricultural product.
▷ Near the town of Wasco, a grain elevator stands amidst wheat fields.
▷▷ A crescent moon rises over America's largest nighttime ski area, Ski Bowl, located at Government Camp.

◁ Mount Jefferson, rising to 10,497 feet, is visible from the top of Mount Hood Meadows' highest lift, the Cascade Express. Mount Jefferson is situated in the Cascade Range some seventy miles southeast of Portland.
△ The Flag Point forest fire lookout, in the Barlow Ranger District, is available for rentals from November to April.

△ A deer ventures out to a clearing at Mitchell Point. Several tunnels were cut through Mitchell Point as part of the Historic Columbia River Highway, the only highway through the Columbia River Gorge on the Oregon side before construction of Interstate 84.

△ Hundreds of raptors, including merlin falcons (also known as pigeon hawks), are counted and released by volunteers at the annual Bonney Butte HawkWatch event in October.

△ Julio Viamonte enjoys telemark skiing on Cooper Spur. Originating in
Norway, telemark skiing is distinguished by a technique for making turns.
Cooper Spur is on the majestic north side of the mountain.

△ A family skis in to the picturesque Summit Meadow Cabins, located near Government Camp, for a weekend of rest, relaxation, and recreation.
▷▷ A rainbow hugs the forest slope at Bluegrass Ridge.

△ Wy'east, the legendary chief of the Multnomah tribe, reveals his face and headdress near the North Face summit of Mount Hood. Only when snow and light conditions are just right is it possible to see his features.
▷ The moon sets over Illumination Rock, on the mountain's southwest side. In 1845, desperate to reach the Willamette Valley before winter, Joel Palmer climbed to Illumination Rock to scout an overland route.
▷▷ A full moon rises over the cloud-obscured west face of Mount Hood.